EGO DYNAMICS

UNDERSTAND YOUR EGO, PRIDE, ATTITUDE & SELF ESTEEM

DR. D. S. NEPRAM

ISBN 979-888569916-7

Dedicated to my parents.

Contents

Acknowledgements

First of all, I sincerely acknowledge with thanks all the readers for their support, encouragement, and honest feedback which give me motivation and inspiration. I would also like to thank my teachers, mentor, well-wishers, and friends who always guided me in the right direction. I would also like to thank the publisher team and experts who helped me in publishing this book. Lastly my heartfelt gratitude to my wife and daughters for unconditional love and care for me.

CHAPTER ONE

What is EGO

*****

"When the Ego dies, the soul Awakes"

-Mahatma Gandhi

We the human being are different from the animal kingdom mainly on the social and ability for higher thinking. We also identified ourselves as a unique people from other human beings. We give our identities which are associated or attached within our mind. It may be name, religion, caste, nationality, color, sex, etc. Further, we also identified with our achievement and our professions which are acquired over the years. The experiences we had in the past which are stored in our minds also help in constructing our own identity. This mental projection of self out of our mind memories and the mental frame is nothing but EGO.

You might have heard the story of a sculpture. Let me tell you the gist of this interesting story. Once upon a time, there was a sculpture. He was very popular and famous for his unique skills in sculpture. He can make exact replicas/ statues of different peoples. He was very proud of his skills. One day, an astrologer visited his house and shows his palm. The sculpture requested to see his palm to predict the future. The astrologer looked at him and told him that he will die within 15 days. The sculpture was very afraid and nervous. After lots of thinking, he came out with an idea that he will make five numbers the same to him to confuse the GOD of death. On the 15th day night, the GOD of death came to his house and show the 6 nos. of the sculptures which were laying on the bed. The GOD death was confused as all the six were the same and identical. He could not identify the real person. Then, the GOD of death got an idea to identify the real one. He said that I appreciate the skills and arts of making this sculpture but there is one small mistake in all the statues. Had the sculpture been there I could have told him about where the mistake was. After hearing this, the sculpture who was also lying in the bed suddenly got up and said I make it all perfect the same as me. What a mistake I have done. The GOD of death replied that the only mistake is your ego which has to awaken up you. Finally, he died because of his ego.

The "I" ness:

You probably heard about the ego, egoistic, positive, or negative side of ego. How could it relate to our life? I am sure you might have heard people talking about problems of ego. Let us talk about ego and understand the concept of ego and its relation to the success of life.

When one says things like *"I am a security guard", "I am a technologist", "I am a CEO", "I am homeless", "I am a parent", "I am a writer", "I was betrayed", "I am a sufferer of some disease"* +etc., this is part of identification with the mind or mental conditioning[1]. This means thinking or taking that role or label or story, which are no more than a bunch of thoughts attached to the primordial 'I' and its other thought forms, are you. In more direct words, you become your thoughts, reactions, and emotions. That's what *'mind-identification'* implies in this context.

Egois the Latin word for "I.". Ego is a self-generating identity every belief about who and what we are. This includes our personalities or talents and our likes and dislikes. The ego keeps us locked away in our minds in an endless cycle of chatter separated from the present moment. It is the identity created and reinforced by the stories we tell ourselves. Our stories are however just stories and they do not make up who we are. Ego is that aspect of yourself, it is you is the self-image of you and it is a self-construct image deep in mind.

The ego is like a mirror that reflects our image. Image in the mirror is what we are however, we are not the image. Our images in the mirror vary from time to time depending on what we dress up and the type of mirrors upon which we see ourselves. Sometimes, we look good and sometimes we look bad, sometimes we look funny. Is not it so?

The ego derives its sense of self from a bundle of thoughts and feelings attached to status, conditions, culture, physical appearance, relationships, gender, experiences, stories, knowledge, history, etc. "Better" or "worse" the label or story or condition, stronger the identification. Ego says: ‘I have, therefore I am. And the more I have, the more I am and vice versa. This delusion is the opposite of the truth.

Ego is that aspect of yourself that you considered in you, that you what I mean is your name, that is me, ego is the self-image of who you are. It is a self-construct image deep in mind. Ego in simple terms can be referred to as I, Me, and Myself. Your *ego* is your conscious mind, the part of your identity that you consider your "self."

Mental Construct of Self Being:

The ego is a complex construct of self in the mind. So ego is that you think you are. It is the thoughts and the emotions that you are identified with. It is the belief that you are rock solid and completely true. It is whole you think the reality is like so that whole construct and it is a very big deep construct. It is like a gigantic iceberg. Only the tip of it like the 10% of it is sticking out of the water and the other 90% are submerged and you don't know what they are is just operating is just working.

It separates itself from everything else out in the world. So you have a very clear separation this is something that you get as a biological entity as an organism that needs to survive and depends on survival and reproduction. So we as a species sense of I ness i.e. this is me. This is what is important and the other kinds of stuff are not so important. If you are trying to get to higher levels of achievements and success in your life, the ego tends to hold back because it got a lot of inertia and weight to it and it doesn't always want to go out there and explore reality for what it the reality is. Because what happened is that ego has been built up regardless of how attached you are to yourself right now the fact is you and notion of you is highly illusory and fictitious. The ego does not want to hear it but it's is the very arbitrary way in which the ego come about it just come about through the experiences that you had in early childhood and then early adulthood up to now and every experience that you had in your whole life from birth to his current day. What is created is a giant yarn ball of all these different strands all tightly interwoven. Now it is like an object. Got its mass to it. It is hard to pull a strand out and create something useful, something that going to get you a better level of performance. Personal development is about is working with the ego.

Personality and Relationship:

The ego is often interpreted as the sum of one's subjective ways of identifying oneself in distinction to the environment. In psychology, the ego is usually a conception about traits of thought, emotion, and behavior that serve to protect, develop and grow the personality. It came to be used to refer to those desires of a possessive or 'selfish' origin, as most easily seen in attitudes, behavior, and reactions that aim to defend and strengthen oneself about any perceived threats. The ego or structure of functioning personality living in the world is an unavoidable part of the human make-up. It is not a static entity but develops and changes in various ways through life.

Some people think of ego as self-respect. Though it is true in some cases, it can often lead to arrogance unconsciously. Ego is a feeling of being superior to others. It originates in the mind and has often no relation with reality. A person who keeps thinking about himself all the time has a larger ego than a person who is concerned about others.

The ego acts as a hurdle when one tries to develop a positive relationship with another person. It also stops one from saying sorry to another person as ego gets hurt in the process. The ego is self-intoxicating and you provide it nourishment every time you think of yourself as superior to others. A bloated or super-sized ego is harmful to a person as he can never adjust with others since he thinks about his superiority all the time. Ego is, therefore, an unhealthy pride that leads to arrogance. Ego gives one a swollen head, which always causes problems[2].

An egotistic person can be someone prone to talking about themselves frequently or someone who appears vain or boastful. It can also be used to indicate someone opinionated, self-centered, or selfish, as well. As you can imagine, being in a relationship with an egotistic person can have its challenges. If you feel you are dating an egotistic individual, work towards dealing with the egotism in the relationship. It is also important to communicate your needs to your partner and make sure you are taking care of yourself.

Egotism and Narcissism:

How would you define *egotism* to an average person? What traits do the egotists you've met display? How do you feel around someone who is *egotistical*? How do you respond to them - with annoyance? Irritation? Repressed or overt disapproval? Scorn? Compassion? Amusement? Tolerance? Avoidance? What needs in you are not met well when you encounter an egotist - especially one whom you're forced to relate to, like a boss, in-law, or co-worker?

*Egotism*refers to often focusing on yourself and ignoring or minimizing other people, without guilt or apology, valuing your talents and achievements above other people's, and minimizing or ignoring other people's needs, talents, and gifts. *Grandiosity* is a form of egotism where a person needs to distort reality and see themselves and their actions as significantly superior to other people.

Egotists can overreact to criticism, becoming angry, defensive, contemptuous, belligerent, and/or blameful. They may have trouble listening to opinions that differ from theirs and acknowledging other people's rights as being equal to their own. They may or may not be rigid and prejudiced about some ideas or people, preach and moralize, and/or may interrupt to focus on themselves. If egotists' monolog about themselves, they may be boring, and they may have an irritating sense of entitlement.

Paradoxically, egotism is often an unconscious defense (protection) against a profound feeling of worthlessness (shame). Typical egotists are psychologically wounded people with no concept of their wounds, what they mean, and what to do about them. They were probably shamed as young kids, or excessively praised and spoiled by insecure, shamed parents.

Narcissism comes from the mythological Greek Narcissus, who fell in love with his reflection in a pool. Both Narcissists and egotists focus mainly on themselves. The former says "I *adore myself! The latter* says "I am better than you,"

The media and the Web generally demonize "*Narcissists,*" depicting them as menacing predators who are conniving, controlling, selfish, dishonest, arrogant, manipulative, insensitive, and abusive - i.e. asserting that they arebad people meriting scorn, hostility, criticism, and disgust. This pejorative attitude blocks effective communication with these injured people and *amplifies* relationship problems with them.

Narcissistic traits are real. They stem from inherited psychological wounds and unawareness from early-childhood abandonment, neglect, and abuse (trauma). Typical survivors are unaware of this toxic inheritance or deny it. Because Narcissistic traits are caused by distrustful false selves, *the person cannot willfully change his or her attitudes and behaviors* any more than an addict can intellectually decide to quit a toxic compulsion. "Will-power" is useless. Egotism and Narcissism are related but have different traits.

The most common ego identifications have to do with possessions, the work you do, social status and recognition, knowledge and education, physical appearance, special abilities, relationships, persons and family history, belief system, often nationalism, racial, religious, and other collective identification. None of these are you.

While the ego is an aspect of the human condition, it is not the true essence of who we are. When we operate from ego we are generally obsessed with right and wrong, blame and shame. We are not acting from a loving place but a judgmental place. We are not acting from a place of how can I serve, how can I give rather what do I get and how do I look. Learning to identify the traits and behaviors of the ego and then working to consciously make a different choice that will drastically change our life.

- **Key Take Away from this Chapter:**

i. The ego is a self-generating identity in our mind that arises out of thoughts, feeling, experiences and attachments. It is a feeling of I, Me, and Myself.

v. Ego is a feeling of being superior to others.

v. Ego is an unhealthy pride that leads to arrogance.

v. The most common ego identifications are family, profession, knowledge, education, nationalities, race, religion, and other collective identification. But none of these are who you are.

CHAPTER TWO

Id, Ego, and Super Ego

"More the Knowledge Lesser the EGO. Lesser the Knowledge more the EGO"

-Albert Einstein

Freudian Psychoanalytical Theory:

The ego is a very interesting concept in psychology. Sigmund Freud is the author of the structural model of personality. In this theory, Freud explains that each person's personality is formed of three parts: i.e. *Id, Ego,* the *Superego*. Psychoanalysis is the process of using what we know about these three parts of someone's personality to analyze the ways that person behaves[3]. The Id and Superego are driven by the pleasure principle and moral principle restrictively. Whereas, the Ego is driven by the reality principle. The ego tries to balance between Id and Superego.

The psychoanalytical theory of Id, ego and superego is explained with the analogy of horse and chariot. An old buggy a horse carriage drew buggy and here you have got the horses which are pulling this buggy forward at breakneck speed. Then you have got the rider on top of the buggy who is holding the reins and trying to control the horses and trying to steer the horses. He is whipping the horses to make them run and that is like the relationship between the ego and the id. The Id is the horse and the ego is the rider. He is trying to control the horses but then inside the carriage behind the rider is his old father and his father is yelling at the rider telling him where to steer the carriage and that is like the superego. So it over this image because it is so easy to remember and it just clearly illustrates what each one of these functions of the psyche is and that is exactly what Freud was talking about. These are functions of the psyche the Id, the ego, and the superego. It is the horse or the multiple horses that you got pulling your carriage forward so that it can be described as your more basic instinctual desires. This is that force within you that force within your psyche that is looking for instant gratification and that is looking for pleasure. It is more or less unconscious in the way you would imagine a horse. A horse is just kind of doing its own thing. It is not too worried about where we are going. It is just hungry or it is thirsty or it wants to run or it does not want to move and that is just a horse.

Then you have got the ego. The ego is the rider. He is the rational one. He is the more conscious one and he is the one who is controlling the horses. He is thinking long-term. He is planning. He is a real person. He is the strategic element of the psyche. He is that part of you that is rational and that is planning your life. That is the ego. It is trying to rein the horses because sometimes the horses want to do crazy things that are not healthy for the overall. It might even be something that is not healthy for the horses themselves. Maybe horses decide that they will go and want to lead the carriage and themselves off the cliff and they will do that unless the rider holds them back and steers them in the right direction.

Then of course we cannot forget the loveable old cranky man the father sitting in the carriage behind the rider. He is the wise one and he is the one who knows best. He got experience and he got morals. He got ideal and he got high standards. He is the societal influence. He is the one who is lecturing who is moralizing the rider on how to best steer the horses so he might criticize the rider in one aspect of how he manages the horses or he might offer some suggestions, some advice about how it should be done better and that is the super-ego.

That is the part of our psyche that is the moralizing part it is our conscience you might say it that part that is the ideal self but also the critical self it is that inner critic that we all have that tells us that we now we could be doing better and that we should be living to something more than we currently are.

So this is the dynamic of the ID, the ego, and the super ego. This is the human psyche. We had this very low basic instinct which is virtual and unconscious the horses but it all it wants are instant gratification and desires right quick hits of pleasure without thinking about long-term repercussions than he imagined. We have got the flip side of the complete opposite which is like moralizing the ideal side of us which knows what should be done. This is the conscious part but it is also the part that can be sometimes too ideal stick to moralizing to sermonizing and so then you have this dysfunction in between which is the ego and it's the job of the ego to kind of guide between the two extremes. The ego is trying to live up to the conscience but on the other hand, it is also trying to appease the horses and it is trying to appease the ID. The ego wants to indulge in pleasures but is not one indulgent pleasure in such a way that it is self-destructive and it is going to lead you off a cliff so he listens to the superego and then sometimes the superego is a little bit too stern and a little bit too self-criticizing too judgmental and so the ego wants to bring it back towards the Id and this is the job of the ego it's to mediate between these two extremes like the best in us and the worst in us. To keep us on the road going forward in life doing whatever it is that we have to do.

The **id** is the "horse". It is the unevolved instinctive part of our brain, responsible for the urges and desires we try to repress.

The **ego** is the "driver" of the chariot and the rational part of our brain. It can guide the id but never has full control - just as the driver is aware that if the horse wants to go in a different direction, he is ultimately powerless to stop it.

The **superego** is the chariot driver's father, sitting behind him, pointing out his mistakes. It is the part of our brain responsible for criticism and moralizing.

All our behavior is ruled by the id because this is where our basic survival instincts are located, and where our desire for pleasure-seeking comes from. As we get older, our ego develops and is shaped by influences in our environment.

The ego is the way human minds balance between the instincts of immediate and delayed gratification of needs. While the Id demands immediate gratification and the superego aims to delay it, the ego finds the right balance between what one wants and what one should.

What is Id?

The id is the instinct that humans possess. The primary goal of Id is gaining satisfaction without giving much thought to anything else. It can be easily defined as the unorganized part of the personality structure that determines a person's basic instinctual drives. Beings the source of a person's bodily needs, Id controls one's desires, impulses, aggressive and sexual drives. It is a selfish nature that everyone possesses which enables humans to take care of themselves. Id is also the part that dislikes pain and cherishes pleasure. Humans are believed to be possessing Id already at birth. That is why the personality of a newborn child is considered to have only Id as it has not been subjected to the ways of the external world. As it grows up with the influence of the external world, this child develops an ego and superego.

The Id is the primitive and instinctive component of personality. The id is the impulsive (and unconscious) part of our psyche that responds directly and immediately to basic urges, needs, and desires. The Id remains infantile in its function throughout a person's life and does not change with time or experience, as it is not in touch with the external world. The Id is not affected by reality, logic, or the everyday world, as it operates within the unconscious part of the mind. The Id engages in primary process thinking, which is primitive, illogical, irrational, and fantasy-oriented. This form of process thinking has no comprehension of objective reality and is selfish and wishful.

The Id is the part of the personality that contains our primitive impulses—such as thirst, anger, hunger—and the desire for instant gratification or release. We are born with our Id. The Id is an important part of our personality because as newborns, it allows us to get our basic needs met. The Id is driven by the pleasure principle, which strives for immediate gratification of all desires, wants, and needs. If these needs are not satisfied immediately, the result is a state of anxiety or tension. For example, an increase in hunger or thirst should produce an immediate attempt to eat or drink. It is also the source of energy, but lacking direction, it needs the superego to help harness it and control it. In popular thought, it is connected with impulse, lust, and "I want it all now" kinds of behavior.

The Id is very important early in life because it ensures that an infant's needs are met. If the infant is hungry or uncomfortable, they will cry until the demands of the id are satisfied. Young infants are ruled entirely by the Id, there is no reasoning with them when these needs demand satisfaction. Imagine trying to convince a baby to wait until lunchtime to eat their meal. The Id requires immediate satisfaction, and because the other components of personality are not yet present, the infant will cry until these needs are fulfilled. However, immediately fulfilling these needs is not always realistic or even possible. If we were ruled entirely by the pleasure principle, we might find ourselves grabbing the things that we want out of other people's hands to satisfy our cravings.

This behavior would be both disruptive and socially unacceptable. The id tries to resolve the tension created by the pleasure principle through the use of primary process thinking, which involves forming a mental image of the desired object as a way of satisfying the need. Although people eventually learn to control the Id, this part of personality remains the same infantile, primal force throughout life. It is the development of the ego and the superego that allows people to control the Id's basic instincts and act in ways that are both realistic and socially acceptable.

What is Ego?

According to Freud, the ego develops from the Id and ensures that the impulses of the Id can be expressed in a manner acceptable in the real world. The ego operates based on the reality principle, which strives to satisfy the Id's desires in realistic and socially appropriate ways. The reality principle weighs the costs and benefits of an action before deciding to act upon or abandon impulses. In many cases, the Id's impulses can be satisfied through a process of delayed gratification—the ego will eventually allow the behavior, but only in the appropriate time and place.

The ego also discharges tension created by unmet impulses through secondary process thinking, in which the ego tries to find an object in the real world that matches the mental image created by the id's primary process. Imagine that you are stuck in a long meeting at work. You find yourself growing increasingly hungry as the meeting drags on. While the Id might compel you to jump up from your seat and rush to the break room for a snack, the ego guides you to sit quietly and wait for the meeting to end. Instead of acting upon the primal urges of the Id, you spend the rest of the meeting imagining yourself eating a cheeseburger. Once the meeting is finally over, you can seek out the object you were imagining and satisfy the demands of the Id realistically and appropriately.

The ego is the part of the personality that maintains a balance between our impulses (our id) and our conscience (our superego). The ego understands that other people have needs and desires and that sometimes being impulsive or selfish can hurt us in the end. It is the ego's job to meet the needs of the Id while taking into consideration the reality of the situation. The ego works, in other words, to balance the id and superego. The ego is represented by a person, with a devil (the id) on one shoulder and an angel (the superego) on the other.

The ego is the only part of the conscious personality. It's what the person is aware of when they think about themselves, and is what they usually try to project toward others. The ego considers social realities and norms, etiquette, and rules in deciding how to behave. The ego engages in secondary process thinking, which is rational, realistic, and orientated towards problem-solving. If a plan of action does not work, then it is thought through again until a solution is found. This is known as reality testing and enables the person to control their impulses and demonstrate self-control, via mastery of the ego.

What is Superego?

The superego is the aspect of personality that holds all of our internalized moral standards and ideals that we acquire from both parents and society, based on our sense of right and wrong. It provides guidelines for making judgments.

The superego incorporates the values and morals of society which are learned from one's parents and others. It develops around the age of 3 – 5 years during the phallic stage of psychosexual development. The superego is seen as the purveyor or rewards (feelings of pride and satisfaction) and punishments (feelings of shame and guilt) depending on which part (the ego-deal or conscious) is activated.

The superego is a part of the unconscious that is the voice of conscience (doing what is right) and the source of self-criticism. It reflects society's moral values to some degree, and a person is sometimes aware of their morality and ethics, but the superego contains a vast number of codes, or prohibitions, that are issued mostly unconsciously in the form of commands or "don't" statements.

The superego's function is to control the id's impulses, especially those which society forbids, such as sex and aggression. It also has the function of persuading the ego to turn to moralistic goals rather than simply realistic ones and to strive for perfection.

The superego has two parts[4]:

I. The **conscience** includes information about things that are viewed as bad by parents and society. The conscience is our 'inner voice' that tells us when we have done something wrong. The conscience can punish the ego by causing feelings of guilt.
II. The **ego ideal** includes the rules and standards for behaviors that the ego aspires to. The ideal self (or ego-ideal) is an imaginary picture of how you ought to be and represents career aspirations, how to treat other people, and how to behave as a member of society. Behavior that falls short of the ideal self may be punished by the superego through guilt. The super-ego can also reward us through the ideal self when we behave 'properly' by making us feel proud.

The superego tries to perfect and civilize our behavior. It works to suppress all unacceptable urges of the id and struggles to make the ego act upon idealistic standards rather than upon realistic principles. The superego is present in the conscious, preconscious, and unconscious. The superego is sometimes represented by an angel sitting on someone's shoulder, telling the ego to base behavior on how the action will influence society.

Interaction of Id, Ego, and Superego:

When talking about the id, the ego, and the superego, it is important to remember that these are not three separate entities with clearly defined boundaries. These aspects are dynamic and always interact to influence an individual's overall personality and behavior. The ego is the psychological component of the personality that is represented by our conscious decision-making process. The Id is the instinctual, biological component, and the superego is the social component of our personality and conscience. Our behavior is determined by the interaction of these three components.

We may say that the id comprises the psychic representatives of the drives, the ego consists of those functions which have to do with the individual's relation to his environment, and the superego comprises the moral precepts of our minds and our ideal aspirations. The drives, of course, we assume to be present from birth, but the same is certainly not true of interest in or control of the environment on the one hand, nor of any moral sense or aspirations on the other.

The Id comprised the entire psychic apparatus at birth. The ego and superego were originally parts of the id which differentiated sufficiently in the course of growth to warrant they are being considered as separate functional entities to adapt or respond to the external world.

What Happens If There Is an Imbalance?

The key to a healthy personality is a balance between Id, ego, and superego [5]. If the ego can adequately moderate between the demands of reality, the id, and the superego, a healthy and well-adjusted personality emerges. An imbalance between these elements would lead to a maladaptive personality. For example, an individual with an overly dominant Id might become impulsive, uncontrollable, or even criminal. Such an individual act upon their most basic urges with no concern for whether their behavior is appropriate, acceptable, or legal. On the other hand, an overly dominant superego might lead to a personality that is extremely moralistic and judgmental. A person ruled by the superego might not be able to accept anything or anyone that they perceive to be "bad" or "immoral."

While the ego has a tough job to do, it does not have to act alone. Anxiety also plays a role in helping the ego mediate between the demands of the basic urges, moral values, and the real world. When you experience different types of anxiety, defense mechanisms may kick in to help defend the ego and reduce the anxiety you are feeling.

The interface between Inner Self and External World:

Part of the Id has been modified by the direct influence of the external world. In psychoanalysis, the ego is considered to be the understanding of the reality of a person. It includes a sense of justice and reality. Ego helps people plan and be more organized for their endeavors. Ego is considered to be the common sense that everyone possesses and is found in each individual. It has the perception of the things around us as well as subconscious thoughts and consists of perceptual, defensive, executive and intellectual-cognitive functions. It is the ego that considers social norms, social realities, etiquette, and rules when deciding how to behave. Ego keeps the Id in check and tries to find ways to satisfy Id's needs without going against the external world.

These three elements (i.e. Id, ego, and superego) work together to create complex human behaviors. Each component adds its unique contribution to personality and the three interact in ways that have a powerful influence on an individual. Each element of personality emerges at different points in life.

The ego is the mediator and moderator, the container of contemporary experiences though not a holder of them (it is made up of moments of 'now'). It is a referee but not a player in the internal drama. The ego is only a player in the sense of manipulating (or trying to) the external world in service of the internal. So human beings are the arena in which two powerful, awesome armies confront each other, with the ego, powerless to limit their energies, engaged in a damage limitation exercise.

- **Key Take Away from this Chapter:**

i. Freud explains that each person's personality is formed of three parts: i.e. *Id, Ego*, the *Superego*. Id is driven by pleasure principle whereas Superego is driven by moral principle. Ego is trying to balance between Id and Superego and is driven by the reality principle.

v. Id is the primitive and instinctive component of personality that responds directly and immediately to basic urges, needs, and desires.

v. The ego operates in realistic ways of satisfying the id's demands, often compromising or postponing satisfaction to avoid negative consequences of society. The ego considers social realities and norms, etiquette, and rules in deciding how to behave.

v. The superego is the part of the personality that represents the conscience, the moral part of us.

v. A balance in the dynamic interaction of the id, ego, and superego is necessary for a healthy personality.

CHAPTER THREE

Ego Development and Strength

"Whenever I climb I am followed by a dog called 'Ego'".

-Friedrich Nietzsche

Once upon a time, a deer was living in a forest near a lake. He looked down his image in the water of the lake. He thought that how beautiful his horn was. So he was so proud of his beautiful two horns. When he looked at his feet he was not happy because it was so ugly. One day, hunters came into the forest and ran after the deer. He ran very fast and hide in bushy areas. So he was saved from his ugly feet. After some time, the hunters came near where he was hiding. He tried to run but was stuck with bushy branched by his horns. He was coughed by the hunters. He thought I was proud of my horns but it trapped me to be killed by the hunters. Whereas he was unhappy about his ugly legs but saved his life once from the hunters.

Many of us, we proud of ourselves for our beauty, wealth, etc. There is no problem with it. However, the problem arises when our pride trapped us and destroys our life. It becomes an obstruction to the path of success.

In the previous chapter, we have discussed the id, ego, and superego. There is a constant fight between two extreme ends i.e. id (immediate need) and superego (social norms) for every situation. The ego has to take favorable decisions balance between conflicting demands of the Id and superego. Therefore, the ego must have certain maturity or strength to handle this conflict between Id and superego. With age, knowledge, and experiences, the ego develops and evolves to handle more complicated conflicting situations.

Ego development

The newborn human infant reacts to but cannot control, anticipate, or alter sources of stimulation, be they external or internal. At this stage, perception is primitive and diffuse, motor activity is gross and uncoordinated, and self-locomotion is impossible. Learning is limited to the simplest type of stimulus-response conditioning.

The infantile ego develops with the external world and reflects (as psychoanalysis has emphasized) the helpless and dependent infant's efforts to alter or alleviate painfully intense stimuli. Mechanisms evolve for controlling tension while seeking means by which gratifications can be obtained, and these mechanisms develop into increasingly complex forms of mastery.

At the outset, perception and motor activity are closely tied, with stimulation immediately provoking motor action. The delay of action, while tolerating the consequent tension, is the basis for all more-advanced ego functions. This delay is prototypic of the ego's role in later personality functioning. The learned separation of stimulation and response allows the interposition of more complex intellectual activities such as thinking, imagining, and planning. By not reacting directly, the ego develops the capacity to test reality vicariously, to imagine the consequences of one or another course of action, and to decide upon future directions to achieve probable ends. The accumulation and retention of memories of past events are necessary for internal processes of thought and judgment. The acquisition of language started during the second and third years, provides a powerful tool for the development of logical thought processes as well as allowing communication and control of the environment.

As the individual continues to develop, the ego is further differentiated and the superego develops. The superego represents the inhibitions of instinct and the control of impulses through the incorporation of parental and societal standards. Thus, moral standards as perceived by the ego become part of the personality. Conflict, a necessary ingredient for the growth and maturity of the personality, is introduced. The ego comes to mediate between the superego and the id by building up what has been called defense mechanisms.

What is Ego Strength?

Ego strength is the ability of the ego to deal effectively with the demands of the id, the superego, and reality. Those with little ego strength may feel torn between these competing demands while those with too much ego strength can become too unyielding and rigid. Ego strength helps us maintain emotional stability and cope with internal and external stress. A person who has good ego strength can effectively manage these pressures, while a person with too much or too little ego strength can be unyielding or disruptive[6].

Where the Id compels people to act on their most basic urges and the superego strives for adherence to idealistic standards, the ego is the aspect of personality that must strike a balance between these baser urges, moral standards, and the demands of reality. When it comes to mental well-being, ego strength is often used to describe an individual's ability to maintain their identity and sense of self in the face of pain, distress, and conflict. Acquiring new defenses and coping mechanisms is an important component of ego strength.

Strong Ego Strength:

A strong ego is exhibited in the following characteristics: objectivity in one's apprehension of the external world and self-knowledge (insight); capacity to organize activities over longer periods (allowing for the maintenance of schedules and plans); and the ability to follow resolves while choosing decisively among alternatives. The person with a strong ego can also resist immediate environmental and social pressure while contemplating and choosing an appropriate course, and strong ego is further characterized in a person who is not overwhelmed by his or her drives (but instead can direct them into useful channels).

A person with strong ego strength approaches challenges with a sense that he or she can overcome the problem and even grow as a result. By having a strong ego strength, the individual feels that he or she can cope with the problem and find new ways of dealing with struggles. People with well-developed ego strength tend to share some essential characteristics. They tend to be confident in their ability to deal with challenges, and they are good at coming up with solutions to life's problems. They also tend to have high levels of emotional intelligence and can successfully regulate their emotions, even in tough situations. These people can handle whatever life throws at them without losing their sense of self.

People with strong ego strength tend to be very resilient in the face of life's difficulties. Rather than giving up in the face of an obstacle, these individuals view such events as tasks to be mastered and overcome. Even when very difficult events or tragedies occur, those who possess ego strength can pick themselves up, dust themselves off, and move forward with a sense of optimism.

Weak Ego Strength

On the other hand, those with weak ego-strength view challenges as something to avoid. In many cases, reality can seem too overwhelming to deal with. Individuals with low ego strength struggle to cope in the face of problems and may try to avoid reality through wishful thinking, substance use, and fantasies. Weak ego strength is often characterized by a lack of psychological resilience. In the face of life's challenges, those with weak ego strength may simply give up or break down.

On the other hand, the weakness of the ego is characterized by such traits as impulsive or immediate behavior, a sense of inferiority or an inferiority complex, a fragile sense of identity, unstable emotionality, and excessive vulnerability. Perception of reality and self can be distorted. In such cases, the individual may be less capable of productive work, because energy is drained into the protection of unrealistic self-concepts, or the individual may be burdened by neurotic symptoms. Ego weakness also underlies the inflated sense of self, which can be associated with grandiosity and a superiority complex.

- **Key Take Away from this Chapter:**

i. Ego strength is the ability of the ego to deal effectively with the demands of the id, the superego, and reality.
v. Ego strength helps us maintain emotional stability and cope with internal and external stress.

v. A person with a strong ego can also resist immediate environmental and social pressure while contemplating and choosing an appropriate course.

v. Weakness of ego is characterized by such traits as impulsive or immediate behavior, a sense of inferiority or an inferiority complex, a fragile sense of identity, unstable emotionality, and excessive vulnerability.

CHAPTER FOUR

Ego and Pride

"The Ego is not who you are. The ego is your self-image, it is your social mask, it is the role you are playing, your social mask thrives on approval. It wasn't controlled and it is sustained by power because it lives in fear."

– Deepak Chopra.

During my school days, I have learned a poem called the PRIDE. I really could not remember the name of the author. It stuck into my mind which helps in shaping my life till today. Though I could not remember the full text of the poem, I would like to share some of the text which is stilled fresh in my mind. I hope it will be helpful to you too. The poem goes like this.

Who is the Richest?
Who are the Healthies?
Who is the Most Beautiful?
Who is the most Knowledgeable?
Who is the Most Powerful?
All will go away.
When the time comes.

As the rose is prideful of its beauty, it has a thorn in its stem.

As the gold is prideful of its preciousness, it is beaten up many times by a hammer.

As the bamboo tree is prideful of its height, the crow sits on its top.

The above poem is very simple but has deep meaning. It is very much applicable in our life. If we are too much showing our pride, one day it will sure to fall. However, if we are aware of our ego and control our pride, its potential energy can be used or directed to betterment in our life as well as to our society. You may be thinking that ego and pride are the same. It is not the same. There is a subtle difference between ego and pride. Pride is the mental position /image of ourselves out of our achievements or acquired skills.

It is positive energy that gives us to boost up to face challenges and confidence to face difficult times. However, over pride is not good. Too much show up of pride is not good to others. Once you have spoken too much about yourself to others, it is not good as it loses your latent energy. It is also understood that you bosting or showing superiority or ego to others which may hurt their feelings. In other words, ego is the over pride or show up of pride affected our relationship in personal as well as in our professional life.

According to psychology, our mind has three stages preconscious, conscious, unconscious mind. Our mind is full of memories of our past experiences and feelings or thought process. It is just like the tips of icebergs where more than 90% are under bennet the water. Most of our actions, reaction, and behaviors are controlled or influenced by these unconscious minds or memories. Only a conscious mind is reflected to take a conscious decision in day-to-day activities. Our nature or behaviors is shaped by these unconscious minds.

What is Pride?

Pride is an emotional response or attitude to something with an intimate connection to oneself, due to its perceived value. Oxford defines it as "the quality of having an excessively high opinion of oneself or one's importance". This may be related to one's abilities or achievements, positive characteristics of friends or family, or one's country[8].

Pride is an emotion that arises as a result of one's achievements, success, or qualities or properties that are admired by others[9]. Pride brings satisfaction and pleasure to oneself. Pride is also a type of admiration for one's performance or personal traits. This emotion can be viewed both negatively and positively. If an individual feels so high and proud about attainment and feels that he/she is superior to others, pride works negatively. When this happens, the particular individual may not feel like talking and hanging out with others but may prefer to be alone. When pride is taken as a positive trait, it acts as a motivating factor. If an individual is proud of his/her performances, he/she may always try to improve them. Pride, in a way, paves the way to success too.

Moreover, pride is associated with self-satisfaction and self-importance. A person may truly feel proud of his/her skills and accomplishments and this invariably leads to self-confidence as well. A person can be proud of someone else's achievements or success as well. For example, a mother may feel proud of her child if the child achieves something important. So, pride is not a result of self-obsession and may sometimes arise due to others as well.

Pride is a feeling of satisfaction arising from what one has done or achieved. It is a sense of accomplishment that is healthy and good for a person and motivates him to be doing better all the time. A person who takes pride in the quality of his work is never satisfied with a below-par performance and strives to do well all the time.

What is Ego?

Ego is sometimes interpreted as self-esteem or self-respect too. However, the ego is responsible for showing one of his/her identities. Ego is all about I, Me, and Myself. Negative qualities such as excessive pride, vanity, self-importance are also associated with ego. When one thinks too much about oneself, he/she can be said to have a stronger ego than a person who thinks about others. Ego may also lead to arrogance. When a person has an extremely strong opinion about him/herself, it could affect personal relationships as well. This might prevent a person from appreciating, apologizing to another person as it may hurt his/her ego. Thus, ego mostly hurts an individual. However, ego may be considered as positive in an individual if he or she does not allow it to control their life.

What is the Difference Between Ego and Pride?

The words ego and pride are so close in meaning and so interrelated that sometimes it becomes difficult to differentiate between them. If you ask a person the difference between these two concepts, he will in all probability draw a blank. There is a subtle difference between ego and pride though it is often used interchangeably by many. However, these two words are interlinked since they refer to the state of mind of an individual. Ego can be defined in simple terms as the way how a person perceives him/herself. That is how the particular individual thinks, feels, and distinguishes him/herself from the rest. Pride, on the other hand, is a feeling one may get after an accomplishment or success of oneself and someone else. This is the main difference between ego and pride.

Pride, unlike the ego, is a feeling of pleasure and joy. It is a sense of accomplishment that tends to bring humility to a person. You must have noticed how humble those who achieve everything in their field become. Pride gives a swollen heart, unlike the ego, which gives a swollen head. A big heart gives nothing but humility. Ego is born in the mind. Pride is born in the heart. Ego is self-admiration whereas pride is self-satisfaction. Ego leads to arrogance whereas pride leads to humility. Ego results in arrogance most of the time. Whereas pride usually leads to self-satisfaction and sometimes motivation.

Ego arises solely because of one's self. Pride could arise due to own self or somebody else too.

Ego usually forbids individuals from apologizing, appreciating others, and making new friends. Pride sometimes makes others feel motivated about something. A strong ego could be hurt very easily whereas pride usually leads to disappointment.

Excessive pride is one of the deadly sins for a reason. It closes our minds to learning, makes us selfish, and jeopardizes our roles as leaders and successful business owners. But putting pride aside can help us in our endeavors to be better and more successful. Whether you're hearing something new from an intern, an in-law, or a child, there are lessons to be learned every day from people you'd never expect. As Vernon Howard said, "Always walk through life as if you have something new to learn and you will." As you work to become less prideful and a better leader, employee, and business owner, cut yourself some slack. It's never easy to change for the better, but when you put in the work to check your pride at the door, you'll be amazed at the doors it opens and who's waiting to teach you something new.

- **Key Take Away from this Chapter:**

i. Pride is an emotion that arises as a result of one's achievements, success, qualities, or properties that are admired by others.

v. Ego is self-admiration whereas pride is self-satisfaction. Ego leads to arrogance whereas pride leads to humility and sometimes motivation.

Over pride is one of the deadly sins for a reason. It closes our minds to learning, makes us selfish, and jeopardizes our roles as leaders and successful business owners.

CHAPTER FIVE

Ego and Attitude

"Change your attitude and you change your life. You cannot control what happens to you in your life, but you can always control how you respond to it. The way you choose to respond is a reflection of your attitude. By changing your attitude, you also change your perspective and change your life."

—Roy Bennett

You might have probably heard about the story of three envelopes. Let me narrate the short version of this popular story throughout the business world. It concerns a newly appointed young director, for the first time with that magic word 'Director' in the job title. Being somewhat nervous about the step, the advice of an experienced director has sought the person being replaced, who was moving on to some distant and murky part of the hierarchy. "Don't worry" was the reply. "I knew you would ask that question. On your desk, the drawer has three envelopes, marked 1, 2, and 3. You will have three crises in results, and when they happen, just open the appropriate envelope, and you will find the answer to all your problems".

At the end of the first year, results were poor, and the new director was severely hassled by the CEO. Opening the first envelope revealed the message "*Blame the last incumbent*". The director produced a report, which pointed out that it was the policies and practices of the previous incumbent that had caused all the performance problems, and the submission of the report relieved the pressure, until the next end of year results, which were again poor. To head off the inevitable pressure, a new report was produced in line with the contents of the second envelope – "*Reorganize*". This suggested that the director had bottomed out the underlying causes of the performance problems, which were related to an inherited organizational structure that was fundamentally out of step with the current needs of the business. Another year's respite followed. Opening the third envelope a year later completed the cycle - it contained the inevitable message – "*Prepare three envelopes*".

We always often blame others for problems though problems arise from within the self. It is a fight between the inner self and the outside world.

What is Attitude?

Attitude is a psychological construct, a mental and emotional entity that inheres in or characterizes a person[10]. They are complex and are an acquired state through experiences. It is an individual's predisposed state of mind regarding a value and it is precipitated through a responsive expression towards oneself, a person, place, thing, or event which in turn influences the individual's thought and action.

Attitude can also be defined as a mental or neural state of readiness organized through experience influencing dynamically or directly the individuals' response to all objects and situations with which it is related. Some others have said that attitude is a learned or more or less organized tendency to respond persistently usually negatively or positively regarding some situation, idea, object, or class of such objects.

Attitude refers to a feeling, or opinion considering a person, thing, or any substance, that is created in our minds. They could be positive, negative, neutral, or even destructive. Our attitude towards something determines how much we like or dislike that particular thing. Attitudes could be implicit as well as explicit. They are implicit when we are not aware of it in our conscious mind, but they still affect our actions and emotions, while it is explicit, when we are aware of what feeling affects a particular action of ours.

A good attitude leads to the formation of a better personality, beliefs, and in turn good actions. Every person has a particular attitude and helps him to create his own identity and guides his actions. There are a lot of factors that help form a particular attitude like social factors, family, prejudices, personal experiences, social media, educational or religious institutions, or even economic and occupational statuses.

Formation of Attitude:

Attitudes are not biologically inherited but built out of continuous experiences of the world around us. They are the outcome of complex functions of both cultural and functional factors. From birth onwards, every individual is exposed to direct and indirect stimuli of the environment which teach him to hold certain ideas, values, and beliefs.

Initially, the infant being only concerned with the satisfaction of his basic needs like food and care is socially blind and is not concerned about the social sanctions. Through the process of need satisfaction, the child gets a scope to develop an attitude. Those objects and persons which satisfy his needs, he develops a favorable attitude towards them. But when an object or person stands in the way of his need satisfaction, an unfavorable attitude develops towards it.

When the child goes to school, certain values and disciplines are imposed upon him and these values gradually become the core of attitude formation. In the beginning, the child's mental level is less matured, his values are shapeless and the attitude formation is in a completely defused stage. To all these objects, he will simply say like or dislike but he cannot discriminate. At this stage, there is no selectivity of perception which is necessary for the formation of attitude. This selectivity of perception and values gradually grows in children out of which attitudes are formed. This is called differentiation to the objects or stimuli around him which grows in years. These clear-cut differentiations in years indicate that attitude undergoes development in a social context depending upon its existing cultural pattern and social sanctions. After differentiation integration of different value structures and attitudes which encompass them take place. This gives a direction to any attitude. As the child gets maturity by power, prestige, recognition, social approval, rewards, and punishment, he gradually attends to the social world.

In daily life, many of our attitudes are formed based on shortcut values and dictums coming from other people before we make up out- minds ourselves through actual contact with the situation, person, or object. Personal attitudes may develop out of one's interaction, contact, and firsthand experience with the attitudinal objects and other objects related to them.

What is the difference between EGO and ATTITUDE?

Both the words attitude and ego could be used interchangeably and misunderstood sometimes, while they differ a lot. While attitude is a person's thoughts about others, the ego is a person's thoughts about himself. Attitude refers to a person's opinions, emotions, and thinking related to a person or a thing that drives his actions while ego refers to a person's superior thinking about himself. **The main difference between attitude and ego is that** while attitude is a person's opinion about other things or persons, ego is a person's thought about himself. Attitude makes a person think and act differently from others in a good manner while the ego makes a person lonely or aloof from others.

Let us examine the statement - *"I am the king and everyone is my slaves"*[11].

The above quote is very dominant, is not it? If we read it in parts and then we will be able to set the difference between attitude and ego.

In the above phrase, attitude is *"I am the King!"* which helps you to see yourself as you are. It helps to know you and defined yourself. It states your positive approach towards you that may help you to over problems and situations of less self-confidence and self–belief.

While the latter part of the phrase *"Everyone is my slave"*shows ego. Ego is nothing but your approach to others being below or inferior to you. Now you will say that saying "I am the king" also tends to be superior to others, so how come it is not ego. "I am the king" also tends to be superior to others but it does not state that others are inferior to you. Feeling like a King or a Superior person is not the problem but feeling others are inferior to you is what takes you towards the ego.

"I can do it" is attitude whereas *"I can only do it"* is ego. *"I am best"* is attitude whereas *"I am only the best"* is ego. Attitude is a positive mindset whereas ego is a very dangerous mindset. Since attitude is positive it is also the companion of motivation and inspiration too.

A good attitude drives a person's actions in the right direction shapes his personality and makes him feel contended, while ego is never satisfied and will make the person crave for more.

Attitude often arises from a person's inner self and shows us the real intention and how a person is, while ego is a kind of false veil that a person has created for himself where he thinks highly of his abilities and talents. Hence, it is important to have a good attitude to shape up a good personality and boost confidence while not letting ego get onto our heads and build a false world for us.

An attitude of a person usually refers to a predefined way of thinking or feeling about someone or something. While the ego is something more related to a person's mind and refers to his self-esteem or even self- importance.

The difference between Attitude and Ego is that attitude is a kind of mindset or nature of a person that shows how he is and how he deals with a situation, while ego is a kind of superiority feeling or taking pride in your abilities over others.

Attitude can also be called the nature of a person, which varies according to time and situation. Attitude can be both positive and negative. It also works to improve the personality of the person and also to bring down the person. Therefore, it depends on the person, which approach the person chooses. Whether you want to be an ordinary person or a unique person should depend on your attitude. Society will not matter whether you live to exist or not. Whether your future will brighten or darken shall depend on your attitude. It is better to change your attitude and focus on positive things, make your thoughts better, learn always. At the time of learning, keep your attitude right with the people, success will come to your feet.

- **Key Take Away from this Chapter:**

i. Attitude is a mental or neural state of readiness organized through experience influencing dynamically or directly the individuals' response to all objects and situations with which it is related.
v. Attitude may be positive, negative, neutral, or even destructive.
v. While attitude is a person's opinion about other things or persons, the ego is a person's thought about himself.
v. Attitude often arises from a person's inner self and shows us the real intention and how a person is, while ego is a kind of false veil that a person has created for himself where he thinks highly of his abilities and talents.
v. Whether your future will brighten or darken shall depend on your attitude.

CHAPTER SIX

Ego and Self Esteem

"The ego is only an illusion, but a very influential one. Letting the ego illusion become your identity can prevent you from knowing your true self. Ego, the false idea of believing that you are what you have or what you do, is a backwards way of assessing and living life."

-Wayne Dyer

We gain confidence from our experiences and knowledge. We become overconfident when we achieved something extraordinary things and feel proud and happy about it. There is nothing wrong to be happy about it. But the problems arise when we started feeling over pride and showing to others and bossy about it. This overconfidence leads to ego.

Everybody has an ego whether it is big or small is about with whom you are comparing. If you think that you have a big ego means you have bigger egos as compared with the egos of other persons. However, you compare your ego with someone who has a bigger ego than yours, your ego becomes a smaller ego. Therefore, it is all comparative and is very dynamic.

Many times, it does reveal its true color unless or until a situation arises. Many of us are not aware of our egos. We also do not know how big our egos are. The reason being is that our ego triggers when it was hurt or challenged by someone. That means our egos can be awakened by the situation or circumstances encountered by some persons. In that situation, we became more defensive or offensive and our egos insisted and replaced our thought process and started arguing with that person. Otherwise, egos remain in their dormant state. It is like a sleeping giant within our minds. We all experience when are angry and making a heated argument. We take it so personally that we are very angry and your ego started revealing its forms as run the survival or defensive mode. At that time, it became reflexive action and thought.

What is the connection between ego and our emotions? Emotion is also an expression of our feeling or thought in response to certain triggering actions or situations.

What is Self Esteem?

In psychology, the term self-esteem is used to describe a person's overall subjective sense of personal worth or value. In other words, self-esteem may be defined as how much you appreciate and like yourself regardless of the circumstances. Your self-esteem is defined by many factors such as self-confidence, feeling of security, identity, sense of belonging, feeling of competence, etc. Other terms that are often used interchangeably with self-esteem include self-worth, self-regard, and self-respect[12].

Self-esteem has a universal interpretation that is true under all circumstances. It is the value and regard that one has for himself/herself. Self-esteem is the underlying motivation behind all virtues. It is the regard we have for ourselves that guides one's actions. Self-esteem is standing up and treating the self with dignity.

Self-esteem tends to be lowest in childhood and increases during adolescence, as well as adulthood, eventually reaching a fairly stable and enduring level. This makes self-esteem similar to the stability of personality traits over time.

Your self-esteem is an assessment of your self-worth; how much or little are you of value to yourself and others? Your 'self' concept is founded on high self-esteem; what are your self-beliefs (I am confident, I am honest, I am loyal), and do they help you actualize who you want to be in other words, your ideal 'self'? As Maslow argues in his hierarchy of needs one needs high self-esteem to self-actualize and realize one's full potential. We tend to like people with high self-esteem; it is common for these people to be happy, non-needy, and selfless in listening to and helping others. We describe these people as *"down to earth"*.

Why Self-Esteem is important?

Self-esteem impacts your decision-making process, your relationships, your emotional health, and your overall well-being[12]. It also influences motivation, as people with a healthy, positive view of themselves understand their potential and may feel inspired to take on new challenges. People with healthy self-esteem:

- Have a firm understanding of their skills.
- Can maintain healthy relationships with others because they have a healthy relationship with themselves.
- Have realistic and appropriate expectations of themselves and their abilities.
- Understand their needs and can express them.

People with low self-esteem tend to feel less sure of their abilities and may doubt their decision-making process. They may not feel motivated to try novel things because they don't believe they're capable of reaching their goals. Those with low self-esteem may have issues with relationships and expressing their needs. They may also experience low levels of confidence and feel unlovable and unworthy.

People with overly high self-esteem may overestimate their skills and may feel entitled to succeed, even without the abilities to back up their belief in themselves. They may struggle with relationship issues and block themselves from self-improvement because they are so fixated on seeing themselves as perfect.

The concept of self-esteem plays an important role in psychologist Abraham Maslow's hierarchy of needs, which depicts esteem as one of the basic human motivations. Maslow suggested that individuals need both appreciation from other people and inner self-respect to build esteem. Both of these needs must be fulfilled for an individual to grow as a person and reach self-actualization.

It is important to note that self-esteem is a concept distinct from self-efficacy, which involves how well you believe you'll handle future actions, performance, or abilities.

What is Healthy Self-Esteem?

There are some simple ways to tell if you have healthy self-esteem. You probably have healthy self-esteem if you:

- Avoid dwelling on past negative experiences
- Believe you are equal to everyone else, no better and no worse
- Express your needs
- Feel confident
- Have a positive outlook on life
- Say no when you want to

- See your overall strengths and weaknesses and accept them

Having healthy self-esteem can help motivate you to reach your goals because you can navigate life knowing that you are capable of accomplishing what you set your mind to. Additionally, when you have healthy self-esteem, you can set appropriate boundaries in relationships and maintain a healthy relationship with yourself and others.

What is Low Self-Esteem?

Low self-esteem may manifest in a variety of ways. If you have low self-esteem:

- You may believe that others are better than you.
- You may find expressing your needs difficult.
- You may focus on your weaknesses.
- You may frequently experience fear, self-doubt, and worry.
- You may have a negative outlook on life and feel a lack of control.[4]
- You may have an intense fear of failure.
- You may have trouble accepting positive feedback.
- You may have trouble saying no and setting boundaries.
- You may put other people's needs before your own.
- You may struggle with confidence.

Low self-esteem has the potential to lead to a variety of mental health disorders, including anxiety disorders and depressive disorders. You may also find it difficult to pursue your goals and maintain healthy relationships. Having low self-esteem can seriously impact your quality of life and increase your risk of experiencing suicidal thoughts.

What is Excessive Self-Esteem?

Overly high self-esteem is often mislabelled as narcissism, however, some distinct traits differentiate these terms. Individuals with narcissistic traits may appear to have high self-esteem, but their self-esteem may be high or low and is unstable, constantly shifting depending on the given situation. Those with excessive self-esteem:

- May be preoccupied with being perfect
- May focus on always being right
- May believe they cannot fail
- May believe they are more skilled or better than others
- May express grandiose ideas
- May grossly overestimate their skills and abilities

When self-esteem is too high, it can result in relationship problems, difficulty with social situations, and an inability to accept criticism[12].

What are the differences between Ego and Self-esteem?

The ego is the opposite of self-esteem. The problem with the ego is it can often 'disguise' itself as your self-esteem and it is important to become aware of this behavior when it arises. The very basic difference is —ego is negative and counterproductive while self-esteem is positive and a sign of confidence. In self-esteem, the associated feeling is confidence and self-assurance. While in ego the associated feeling is of insecurity and fear. When we are self-assured and confident against a contrasting opinion — it is self-respect. In this situation, we respect our own opinion while giving importance to other opinions as well. But when we have ego then we become in-secured and scared. We close ourselves in a shell thus not respecting others' points of view. Ego leads us to argument, anger, and ultimately to pain and hurt. However, self-respect leads us to stability and peace.

The ego keeps a person in a false world and does not allow the real world of good to be seen. It makes the person have prejudiced or biased thoughts and become judgmental. The ego never gets satisfied and always wants a person to do more. Ego creates a false sense of pride and superiority in the mind of a person resulting in the person over-emphasizing and having overconfidence in his abilities and talents which might not yield good results.

To have confidence is to have faith in your abilities and believe in yourself, but the ego is something else, entirely. Unlike confidence, the ego operates out of self-interest. It seeks approval, accolades, and validation at all costs to be seen as "right". If I love someone and they tell me they don't love me, I realize that not loving me does not make me less worthy of being loved. Me not being loved by another might hurt my feelings but it does not impact my self-esteem. This is because self-esteem is how I see myself, and it comes from inside me.

A person with healthy self-esteem is happy to learn from others, sees herself clearly, and does not link being right or winning with her worth. The relationship between ego and self-esteem is inversely proportional.

Ego is our false self; it is a cover-up for our insecurities. Ego leads us to reject others' opinions which is counterproductive for our development. Ego closes our minds and obstructs our vision so that we cannot see anything other than the ideas of our own.

Self-respect results in personality development and makes the person self-dependent. It stops the person from believing he/she is superior to others, and at the same time it teaches him/her how to value himself/herself. Ego often leads to unhealthy competition and rivalry. It creates an urge to prove oneself even if it is by demeaning others. Ego can destroy relationships, hurt others and make a person isolated in his world. It makes the person emotionally vulnerable and has an impact on his psychological. Self-respect, on the other hand, allows growth, maturity and helps to cultivate self-worth. It is not defensive and improves one's physical, mental, and psychological health.

What are the differences between ego and confidence?

Many of us have the common misconception that ego and confidence are essentially the same things. It's even been said that taking on such an attitude at work will get you ahead in your career[13]. The reality, however, is that these two concepts are quite different. To have confidence is to have faith in your abilities and believe in yourself, but the ego is something else, entirely. Unlike confidence, the ego operates out of self-interest. It seeks approval, accolades, and validation at all costs to be seen as "right". It is resistant to feedback and assigns a motive where there isn't any.

Confidence isn't about feeling superior to others. It's a quiet inner knowledge that you're capable of. Confident people feel secure rather than insecure. They can rely on their skills and strengths to handle whatever comes up. They feel ready for everyday challenges like tests, performances, and competitions. They think "I can" instead of "I can't". Confidence helps us feel ready for life's experiences. When we're confident, we're more likely to move forward with people and opportunities — not back away from them. And if things don't work out at first, confidence helps us try again.

The ego is the part of the person's mind that usually mediates between the conscious and the unconscious and is fully responsible for the real test and sense of personal identity. It is the identity that can prove to be wrong in the end, because in the end, we guess that our identity is artificial. This ego is unique and difficult to see. Because it is hidden behind the opinions that appear to be true which are attached to describe our identity.

Managing Ego:

The best way of managing ego is to break the unhealthy attachment with the self. This unhealthy attachment does not let us appreciate others' points of view. By *"breaking the attachment"* I do not mean to not respect your idea. That will be hurting self-respect. Respect your idea but also listen to others' points of view. By *'breaking the attachment'* I meant to detach ourselves from the behavior causing ego. Respect your opinions but not to the extent that you become defensive.

You have to re-direct your focus on yourself, your 'true', and not your ego or what others may (or may not) think about you. Be honest with yourself, what do you like about yourself and what do you not like about yourself? Do not challenge it — just accept it. The ego is concerned with emphasizing strengths and de-emphasizing weaknesses.

A woman I was speaking to said "you're very arrogant aren't you?" and I said, "no, I'm confident." She said "what is the difference?" and I answered, "arrogance is overcompensating for a known weakness; confidence is knowing your strengths but also knowing your weaknesses, that way you can improve them." There are a lot of people who prefer to 'hide' behind their strengths in fear that if they do not, their weaknesses will be revealed. If you have weaknesses, it is okay, it means that you are a human.

You are not your thoughts. When you become aware of these habitual thought patterns, you begin to become more self-aware of your ego and more importantly, how you can weaken it.

An old Cherokee is teaching his grandson about life. “A fight is going on inside me,” he said to the boy. “It is a terrible fight and it is between two wolves. One is evil — he is anger, envy, sorrow, regret, greed, arrogance self-pity, guilt, resentment, inferiority, lies, false pride, superiority, and ego”. He continued, “the other is good — he is joy, peace, love, hope, serenity, humility, kindness, benevolence, empathy, generosity, truth, compassion, and faith. The same fight is going on inside you –and inside every other person, too.”

The grandson thought about it for a minute and then asked his grandfather, “Which wolf will win?” The old Cherokee simply replied, “the one you feed.”

Some tips to control your ego?

i. Think before you act.
v. Try to see what others feel.
v. Accept criticisms.
v. Admit when you are wrong.
v. Communicate clearly.
v. Do not seek attention.
v. Respect others.
v. Admit when you are wrong.

Some tips to build self-esteem?

v. Love yourself.
v. Believe in what you do.
v. Identify your strengths and weaknesses.

v. Compromise, but wisely.
v. Think positive.

It is argued that ego and self-respect are at the two extreme ends of a continuum. Overdoing self-respect brings in ego. Both ego and self-respect co-exist in each one of us and we must know how to get the perfect balance in them. Self-love and self-confidence are essential for our growth but it should not reach a point where we become selfish and cannot accept reality. It is important to have faith in yourself and be confident with your actions.

- **Key Take Away from this Chapter:**

v. Self-esteem may be defined as how much you appreciate and like yourself regardless of the circumstances.
v. Having healthy self-esteem can help motivate you to reach your goals.
v. Having low self-esteem can seriously impact your quality of life.
v. When self-esteem is too high, it can result in relationship problems, difficulty with social situations, and an inability to accept criticism.

v. Overdoing self-respect brings in ego. Both ego and self-respect co-exist in each one of us and we must know how to get the perfect balance in them.

Self-improvement Exercise

Dear Readers,

If you are serious about taking some benefit out of learning from this book and want to improve your quality of life, please close your eyes and think about yours who you are. Please answer the following questions with honesty and sincerity to yourself.

a). Please write five most likes about yourself.

1.________________________________

2.________________________________

3.________________________________

4.________________________________

5.________________________________

b) Please write five most dislikes about yourself.

1.________________________________

2.________________________________

3.________________________________

4.________________________________

5.________________________________

c) Please write five things that really hurts your EGO

1.________________________________

2.________________________________

3.________________________________

4.________________________________

5.________________________________

d) Please write five things that you think you can really improve upon.

1.________________________________

2.________________________________

3.________________________________

4.________________________________

5.____

e) Please write five most important things that you have learned from this book

1.____
2.____
3.____
4.____
5.____

Reference:

1. Webpage- https://www.wikihow.com/Dissolve-the-Ego-(According-to-Eckhart-Tolle%27s-Teachings)
2. Hasa, *"Difference between ego and pride"*, Webpage: https://www.differencebetween.com/difference-between-ego-and-vs-pride/
3. Freud, Sigmund. *The Standard Edition of the Complete Psychological Works of Sigmund Freud.* Vol. XIX (1999) James Strachey, Gen. Ed. ISBN 0-09-929622-5
4. Webpage: https://www.verywellmind.com/the-id-ego-and-superego-2795951
5. Churchill R, Moore TH, Davies P, et al. *"Psychodynamic therapies versus other psychological therapies for depression". Cochrane Database System Rev.* 2010;(9):CD008706. doi:10.1002/14651858.CD008706.
6. Kendra Cherry,*"The Id, Ego and Superego"*, https://wl.apsva.us/wp-content/uploads/sites/38/2015/06/Id-Ego-Superego.doc
7. Kendra Cherry, "*Characteristic of Ego strength*", Webpage: https://www.verywellmind.com/ego-strength-2795169
8. Webpage: https://en.wikipedia.org/wiki/Pride
9. Chantu, "*Difference between ego and pride*", webpage: https://pediaa.com/difference-between-ego-and-pride
10. Webpage: https://en.wikipedia.org/wiki/Attitude_(psychology)
11. Webpage: https://www.silentmotivations.com/

2018/09/22/difference-between-ego-and-attitude/

12. Kendra Cherry, *"What is Self-esteem?"*, https://www.verywellmind.com/what-is-self-esteem-2795868.
13. Parul Verma, *"Ego vs Self Esteem"*, https://medium.com/@parul26verma/ego-vs-self-esteem-bfe12da0d5e3

Humble Appeal

It is my humble appeal to all the readers to give your honest review of this book to the Amazon book store and another online store. If this book makes some improvement in your life, please share it with others. I will assume that purpose of writing this book has been fulfilled. Your sincere feedback is highly appreciated as it will allow me to improve upon it in my next project.

My best wishes and prayers for your success in life.

9 798885 699167

Printed by Libri Plureos GmbH in Hamburg, Germany